Play
with a PURPOSE

with paper and patterns

BrambleKids

INTRODUCTION

The need for a 'go-to' activity is essential for every busy parent and teacher!

These activities are enjoyable and engaging. They afford valuable learning and development opportunities for children, from physical and intellectual to emotional and social skills. They require only the use of everyday objects, making them perfect for the home or classroom.

Children can work on these fun tasks either independently, with their peers or with adult help.

GET STARTED

All the activities in this book will be easier to manage and protect if they are contained in a safe place. Encourage children to cover a large cardboard box with brightly coloured paper and make it their Paper Box. Different kinds of paper and card can then be kept in it, as well as basic tools such as scissors.

NEW FROM OLD

The theme-based activities in this book afford valuable opportunities to inspire children to learn about RECYCLING. Many of the materials needed are everyday items used in the home that children can turn into something exciting!

These educational crafts will motivate children to keep and reuse many items, such as empty yoghurt pots, jars, kitchen roll tubes and newspapers. They will also teach how to correctly recycle any waste from all activities where appropriate and explain why it is important to do so.

CONTENTS

PAPER PROJECTS

1. You will need — 6–7
2. Make Finger Puppets — 8–9
3. Make a Jigsaw — 10
4. Make a Woven Paper Mat — 11
5. Make a Paper Bead Necklace — 12-13
6. Make a Paper Lantern — 14
7. Make a Crab Chain — 15
8. Make a Zigzag Book — 16
9. Make a Scrapbook — 17
10. Make a Mosaic — 18-19
11. Make Lively Acrobats — 20–21
12. Make Monsters — 22–23
13. Make a Space Mobile — 24–25
14. Make a Clock Face — 26
15. Make a Funny Face Gallery — 27
16. Make Busy Finger Prints — 28–29
17. Make an Underwater Scene — 30–31
18. Make Shadow Puppets — 32-33
19. Make Tube People — 34-35
20. Make a Wriggly Mobile … — 36-37
21. … and a Wrigglier Dragon — 37
22. Make a Secret Code … — 35
23. … and Treasure Hunt Codes — 39
24. Make Drip Patterns — 40
25. Make Comb Patterns — 40
26. Make Handprints — 41
27. Make Wax Patterns — 42
28. Make a Mirror Pattern — 43
29. Make a Suncatcher — 44-45
30. Make a Tangram — 46-47

Take Care!

Some of the activities in this book will require adult supervision. Encourage children to use scissors and pointed utensils with care and in a safe manner, further helping to build their skills and confidence.

Development Links

Physical Skills

* Development of fine motor skills
  All these activities require the movement of hands and fingers. These in turn will involve the use and practice of fine motor skills and the general improvement of muscle control and strength. Developing these skills will extend into everyday activities such as washing and dressing.

* Increase in dexterity
  All these activities require manual dexterity. With practice and time, finer artistic skills will increase.

* Improvements in hand-eye coordination
  These activities require keen hand-eye coordination and such practice will support the development in further areas such as sports.

Intellectual Skills

* Promotion of innovation and creativity
  These activities offer children opportunities to create something new. This will encourage them to think differently and to innovate ideas.

* Development of problem-solving skills
  These activities require children to follow instructions and be resourceful. Encouraging them to work out where they may have gone wrong through discussion will support them in later life.

* Enhancement of decision-making skills
  Solving artistic challenges will promote correct and effective decision-making abilities. This will improve their ability to face other problems.

* Improvement in memory
  These activities require children to use and develop their visualising skills. Visualising complex designs will help improve memory.

* Improvements in visual processing
  These activities require children to identify patterns and colours that will naturally develop visual processing skills. This cognitive development is very important in early years.

Emotional and Social Skills

* **Improvements in self-esteem**
  Encouraging children in these activities will boost their self-esteem. With each completed activity, children will feel a sense of achievement. Creating something allows children to feel in control and confident in themselves.

* **Confident expression of self**
  Artistic activities encourage children to express themselves and your praise and encouragement will give them the confidence to do so. Children can channel negative and positive energy into these activities.

* **Encouragement of creativity**
  Although instructed, all of the activities allow children to use their imagination and turn it into something productive. This will nurture artistic talents and self-esteem.

* **Improvements in working with others**
  Encouraging children to work on these activities with their peers, whether they create a project together or simply support one another, will hugely develop their social skills and abilities. Interacting with other children with the same interests, or working together to overcome differences, will allow for friendships to develop.

* **Strengthen bonds**
  Working together with the child on these activities as a parent or teacher will strengthen your bond. Company will promote the children's enjoyment and engagement with the activity.

1 You will need

This book uses things that are usually found around the house or even things that might normally get thrown away. There are just a few things that might need to be purchased especially.

scissors

ruler

paints

sticky tape

string

paintbrushes

cardboard or kitchen roll

balls of wool

needle and thread

toothpicks or cocktail sticks

A note about glue

There are three types of glue we have used: school glue or paste, PVA and glue sticks. If you are sticking paper and card together, then a glue stick is the best one to use. School glue is best for papier mâché and PVA is best for heavier things, hard surfaces and wool. You can also use PVA as a kind of varnish. If you paint it onto a surface, it will go shiny when it dries.

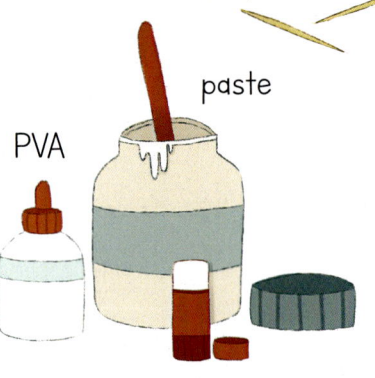

paste

PVA

glue stick

HOW TO MAKE PAPIER MÂCHÉ

Papier mâché is a really fun material to make. It's a mix of paper and glue, or flour and water paste, which hardens when it dries. You can build up layers of paper to mould a vase or a bowl, or scrunch up torn newspaper pieces to make the shape of an animal or person.

Papier mâché takes a long time to dry, so wait before you paint or decorate it.

Things to Remember

If you are covering an object to make a papier-mâché mould, it's best to cover the object in cling film to start with. Use school glue or flour mixed with water into a thick paste. The more layers you add, the firmer your shape will be. Make sure the paper is really soggy with paste for the best results. It won't be waterproof.

sticks or twigs

egg boxes

scraps of material

seeds and rice

lollipop sticks

bowl and old spoon

buttons

comb

2 Make Finger Puppets

You can make all sorts of characters with these finger puppets. Experiment with their facial expressions, from happy to surprised and from silly to scared.

You will need
- Card
- Scissors
- Wool
- Paints
- A brush
- Glue

1 Cut the card into rectangles about 5 centimetres (cm) x 8 cm. Glue the two short ends together to form a tube. Make one for each finger.

2 Paint faces on the front of the tubes and hair on the back. Leave to dry.

3 Cut the wool into lengths, and glue them onto your finger puppets to make hair, beards and moustaches.

3 Make a Jigsaw

You will need

Old cards or card
Coloured pens
Scissors
Envelopes

1 Choose an old greetings card with a colourful picture, or draw a picture of your own onto card. Make sure you cover the whole card

2 Now cut the picture up into about 12 pieces with wiggly lines. Put all the pieces into an envelope.

If there are two of you, you could both make one and then try to make each other's.

④ Make a Woven Paper Mat

You will need

A square piece of card – 18 cm x 18 cm
Coloured paper in two colours –
    also 18 cm x 18 cm
Glue
Scissors
Ruler
Pencil

1 Let's say you have chosen red and blue paper. Measure and rule the red and blue paper into strips 3 cm wide and 20 cm long. Cut along the lines to make 6 strips of each colour.

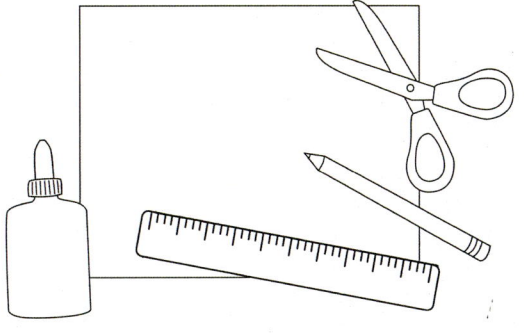
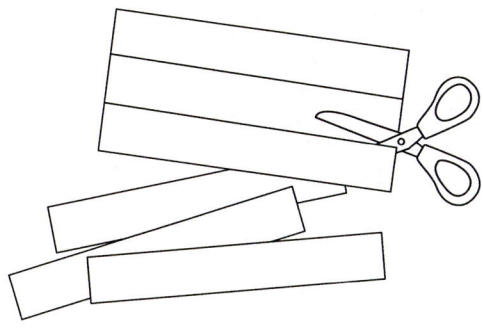

2 Place the strips side by side vertically on top of the card. Fold 1 cm of one end of each of the red strips over the back of the card and glue this bit in place.

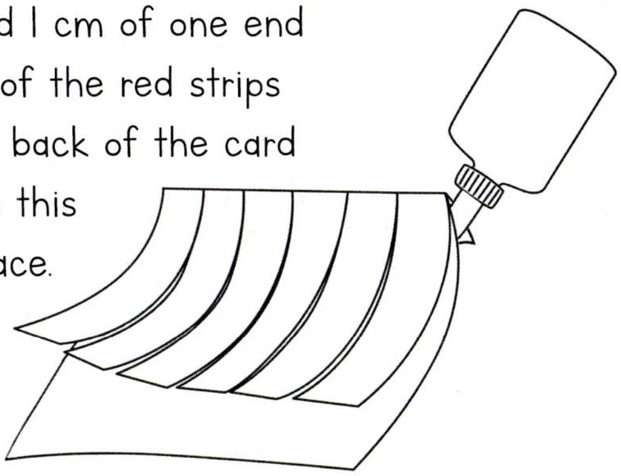

3 Take the blue strips and place them side by side horizontally on top of the red strips. Fold 1 cm of the left end of each of these blue strips over the back of the card and glue them in place.

4 Begin weaving by taking a blue strip and sliding or threading it first over and then under a red strip. Then take the next blue strip and weave it first under and then over the red one. When you get to the end of a row, fold the rest of the strip over the back of the card and glue in place.

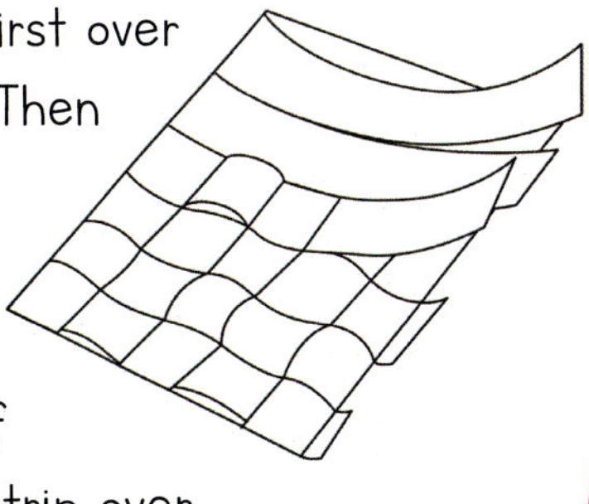

5 Make a Paper Bead Necklace

Make a colourful necklace out of paper for you or your best friend.

You will need

Coloured wrapping or shiny sweet papers
Glue
Pencil
Ruler
Scissors
String

1 Cut the paper into pointed shapes as shown in the picture. Use a ruler to help you get the lines straight.

2 Roll each strip quite loosely around the pencil starting with the wider end and ending at the point. Secure the pointed end with glue. Slide out the pencil to leave a hollow paper tube. Leave to dry.

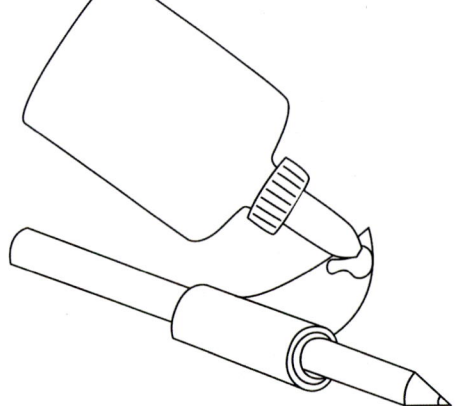

3 Keep going until you have about 60 beads. When you have enough, thread them onto a long piece of string and be sure to tie a good knot at the end.

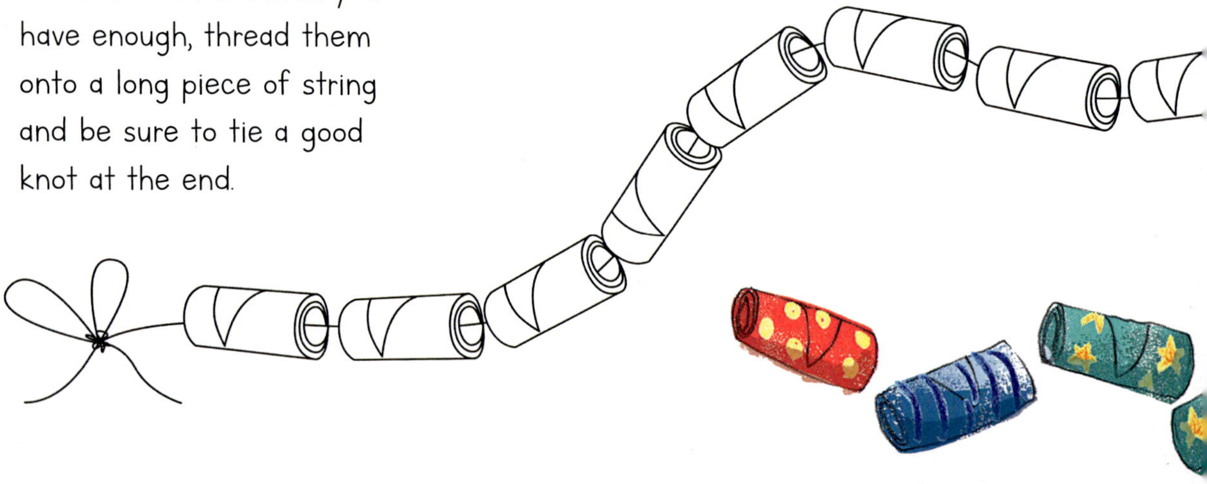

6 Make a Paper Lantern

You will need
Sheet of paper
Coloured pens
Glue
Scissors

1 Cut the paper into an oblong about 20 cm long and 13 cm wide. Fold the paper in half lengthwise.

2 Cut strips in the paper starting at the fold, but be careful not to cut all the way across.

3 Open out the paper and decorate it however you like. When you've finished, bring the 2 short sides together and glue one side over the other.

4 To make the handle, cut a strip of paper and glue each end to the inside of your lantern.

7 Make a Crab Chain

You will need
Pencil
Scissors
Crayons
Paper

1 Fold the paper backwards and forwards to make a fan.

2 Draw half a crab onto the top making sure that half of the crab's body is along the fold and two legs go all the way to the edge.

3 Carefully cut out the crab and then gently unfold your chain of crabs.

15

8 Make a zigzag Book

You will need
A long strip of card   Coloured pencils, felt-tip pens, paints

1 Fold the card in half, and then in half again.

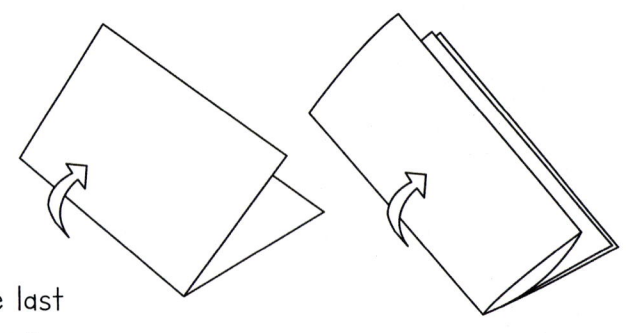

2 Open it up and then refold the last section so that it stands up on it's own in a zigzag.

3 Use the pages of your book to write and illustrate a story that moves through the zigzag pages like one continuous adventure.

9 Make a Scrapbook

You will need

At least 6 sheets of paper all the same size - about 40 cm x 30 cm or larger

Scissors

Needle

Thread

1 Fold each piece of paper in half to form a crease.

2 Open up the paper and place one on top of the other.

3 Thread the needle and tie a large knot in the end of the thread. Sew all the pieces of paper together along the crease using large stitches.

Secure the thread by tying a large knot around the last stitch.

4 Close book you've made and decorate its cover.

TIP You could fill your scrapbook with pictures and stories. Glue in photos, pictures from magazines, or anything that interests you.

You could make this a scrapbook about a holiday or a trip you've been on.

10 Make a Mosaic

A mosaic is a pattern or picture made of little tiles. Ancient Romans made them to decorate the walls and floors of their homes.

You will need

Coloured paper
Card
Scissors
Pencil
Ruler
Glue stick

1 Use the ruler to draw small squares on the coloured paper. Cut them out.

2 Draw a picture on the card and then arrange the squares to fit in the picture.

3 Glue the squares down.

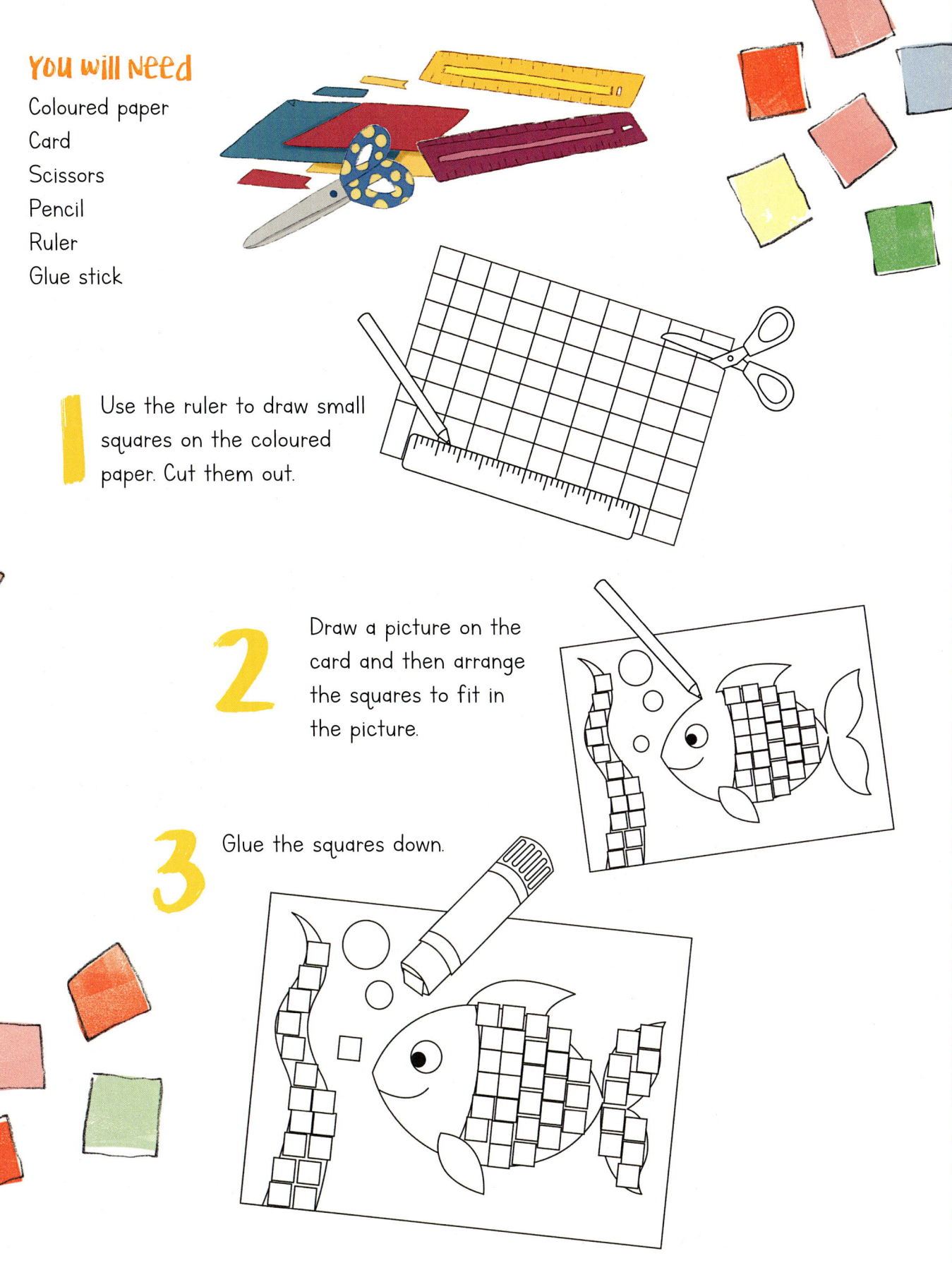

11 Make lively acrobats

You will need
Sheet of white card
Pencil
Coloured felt-tip pens or crayons
Paper fasteners

1 Draw all the body parts on a sheet of card. For each figure you will need a head and body, legs, arms, hands and feet.

2 Decorate the body parts using different colours and patterns.

3 Carefully cut out the separate pieces.

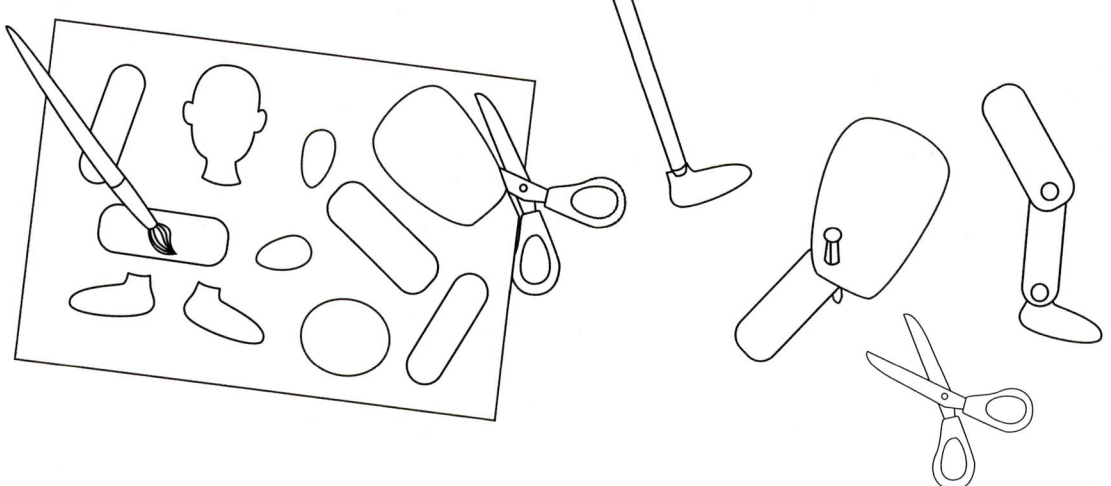

4 Using a sharp pencil point, make holes in the body where each of the parts join. Fix the parts together by linking the holes with paper fasteners.

You can move your acrobats into all kinds of different movements and positions. You can even play some music for them to dance to.

12 Make Monsters

You will need

Coloured and white card
Tissue paper
Pencil
Glue
Scissors
Black marker pen
Paint, foil, sequins, buttons and bottle caps

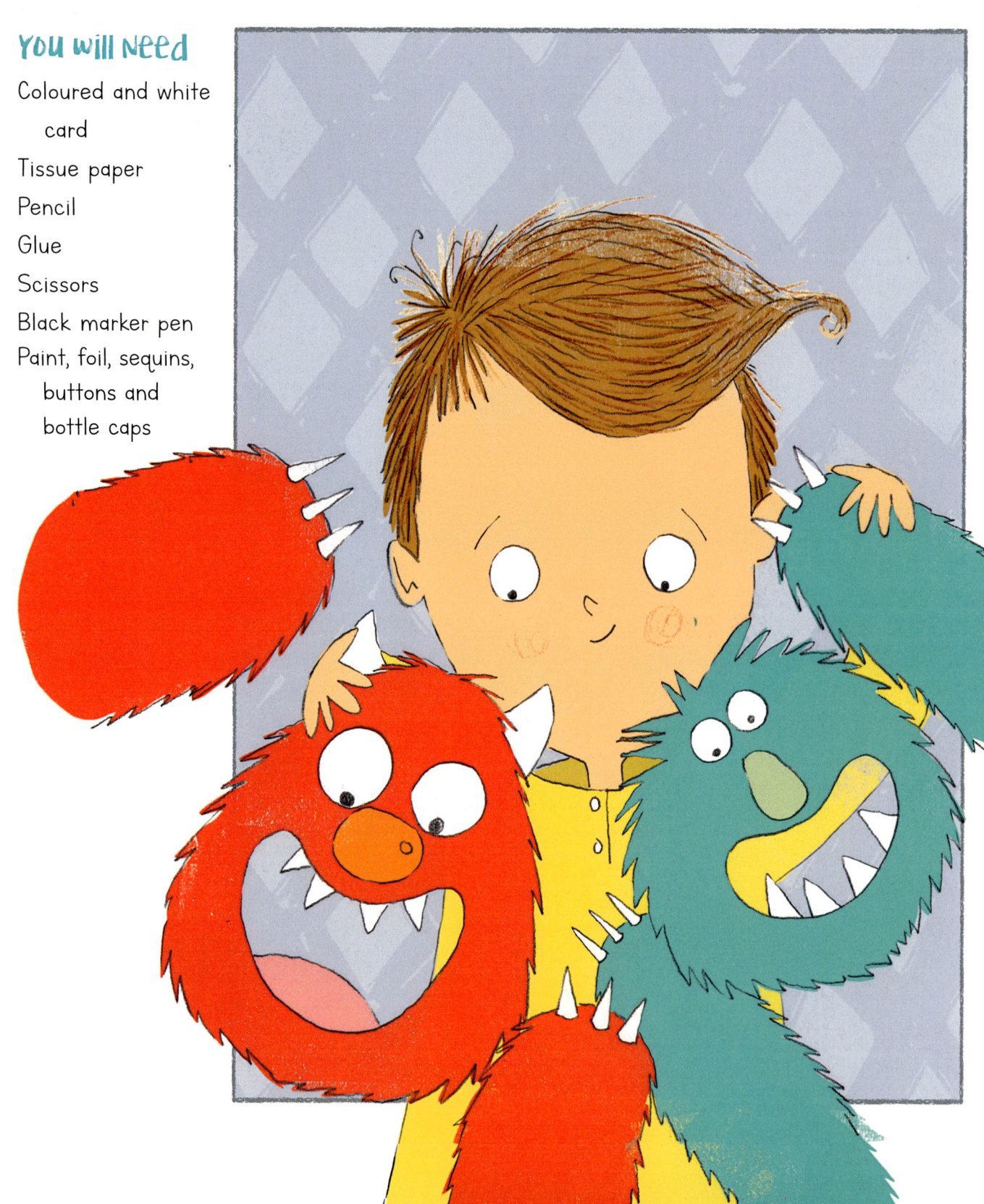

1 Draw the outline of a monster face and hands on a piece of card.

2 Cut out the hands and face, and cut an opening for the mouth.

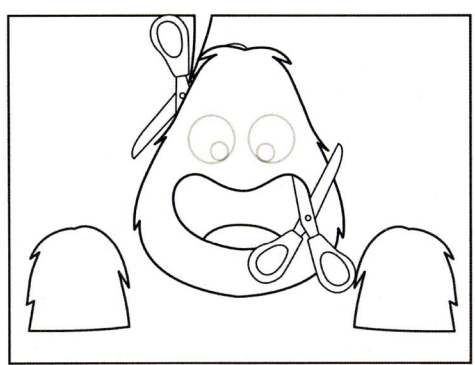

3 Create sharp teeth by cutting triangular shapes from white card. Glue the teeth into the monster's mouth.

4 Cut sharp claws and horns from the card and glue these in place too.

5 Roll up a piece of tissue paper and glue to the card for the nose.

6 Cut shapes from tissue paper and card for the eyes, and glue in place. Use a black marker pen to outline the eyes.

7 Use paint, foil, sequins, buttons, and bottle caps to create different monster faces.

13 Make a Space Mobile

You will need
Lots of newspaper
A bowl of water
School glue
Paints
Brush
Glitter
Big needle
Skewer or kebab stick
Bamboo sticks
String
Aluminium foil
Tape

1 Rip up some of the newspaper into strips and soak them in the water.

To make the Sun, take two large sheets of newspaper and roll them into a big ball. Glue the wet paper strips onto the ball to make a smooth surface.

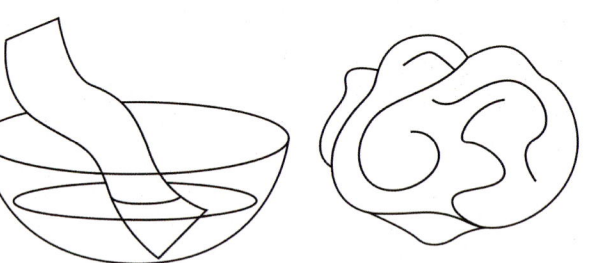

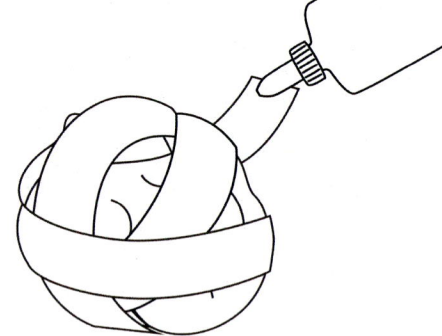

Cover the ball with two or three layers and then leave it to dry.

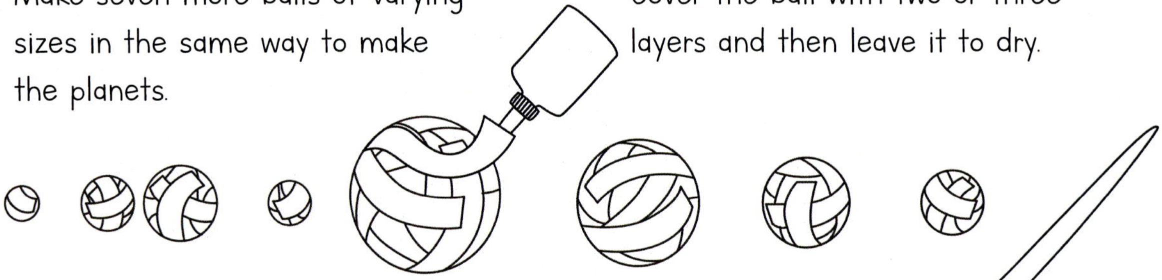

2 Make seven more balls of varying sizes in the same way to make the planets.

3 When they are all dry you can paint them and leave them to dry once more. You can decorate some with swirly patterns or by glueing glitter to them.

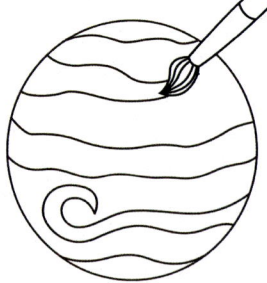

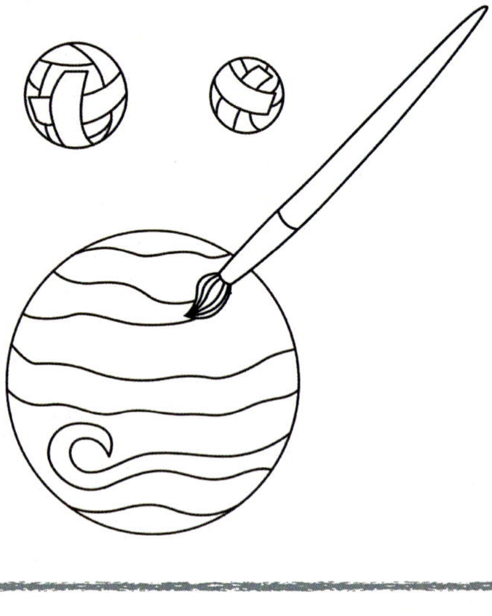

24

4 To assemble your mobile, first tie the bamboo sticks together to form a cross.

5 Push the skewer or kebab stick all the way through the Sun and the planets so each has a hole through its centre.

6 Thread the needle with string and pass it through the Sun. Tie the string together and then tie it to the middle of the bamboo sticks.

7 Thread all your planets in the same way using different lengths of string.

TIP Add some stars by cutting them out of the aluminium foil and sticking them on with tape.

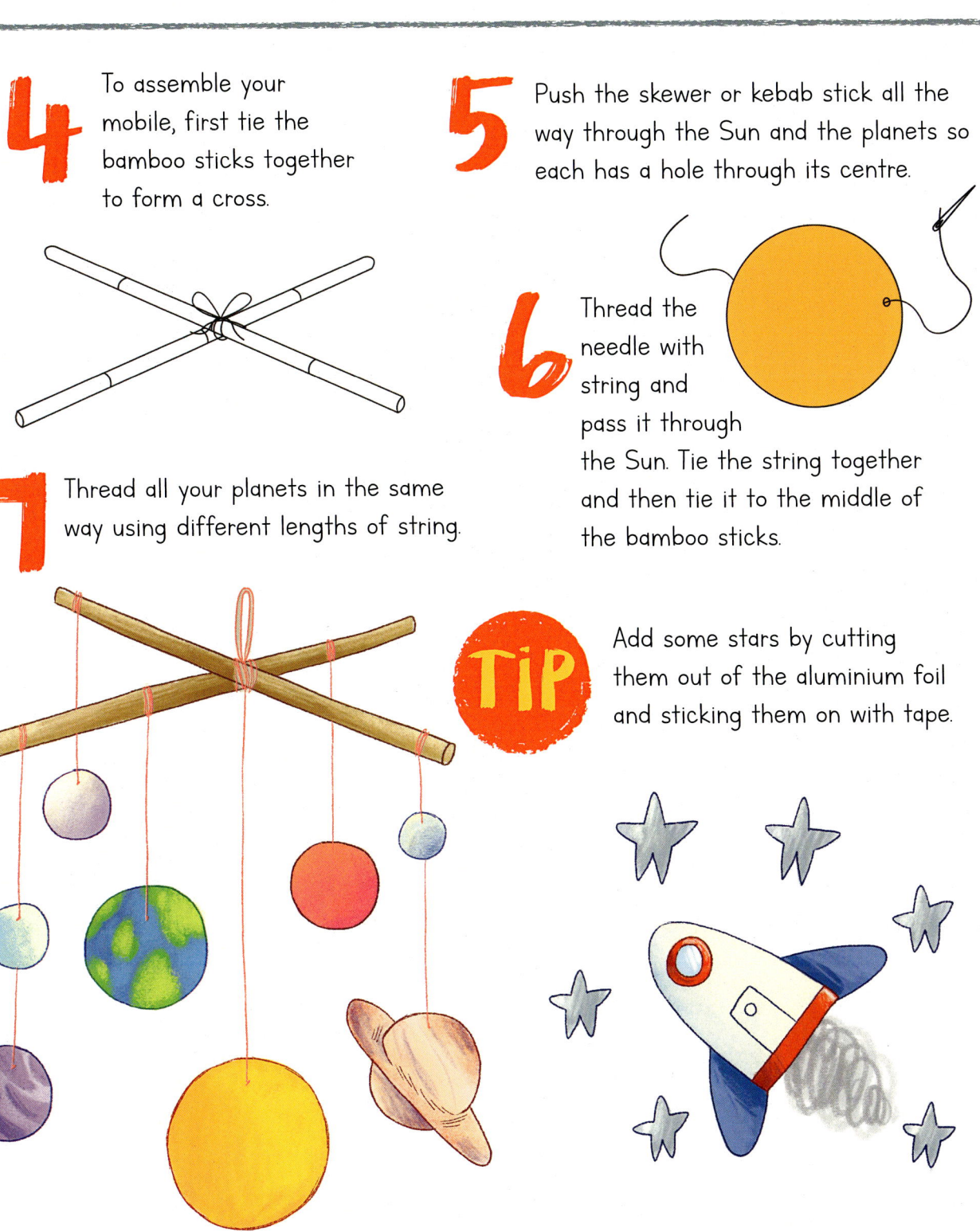

14 Make a clock face

Decide what information you would like on your clock face. Will you use it to tell the time? Or will you use it to remind you of your chores or your lessons?

You will need

- A paper plate
- Scraps of card and coloured paper
- Colour felt-tip pens
- Paper fastener
- Scissors

1 Draw your design on the plate using the felt-tip pens.

2 Cut a hand or a pointer from coloured card and fix one end of it to the centre of the clock face using a paper fastener.

15 Make a funny face gallery

You will need
An old magazine
Scissors
Glue
Paper or card
Pencil
Tape
Lollipop sticks.

TIP Remember to ask permission before cutting up a magazine that doesn't belong to you.

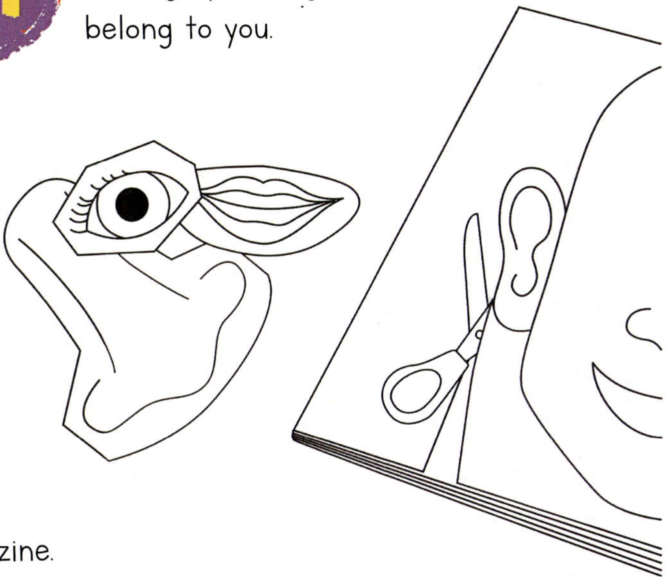

1 Cut out lots of different eyes, noses, mouths, ears and hair from the magazine.

2 Mix them up and glue them onto the paper to make funny face portraits.

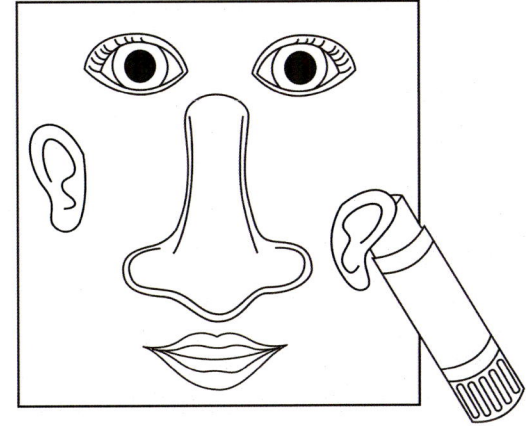

You could also stick them onto a piece of card, cut out the face and stick it to a lollipop stick with a piece of tape to make a mask or puppet.

16 Make busy fingerprints

You will need
Paints
Paint brush
Coloured paper
Black pen

1 Paint your fingertips with paint.

2 Press your fingers onto the paper to make patterns.

3 When they are dry, create insects and animals by drawing eyes, legs and patterns with the pen.

 Make an underwater scene

You will need

- A big piece of card
- Blue, green and turquoise tissue paper
- Coloured paper
- Scissors
- Coloured pencils
- Glue
- Bubble wrap
- Acrylic paint
- Brush

1. Draw some shapes of fish, shells, starfish and rocks on the coloured paper.

2. Cut them out and stick them onto the card.

3. Tear the tissue paper into long strips and glue them over the shapes horizontally. Overlap them so they create different shades.

4. Cut the bubble wrap into long tendrils like seaweed. Paint them different shades of green and stick them onto your picture vertically.

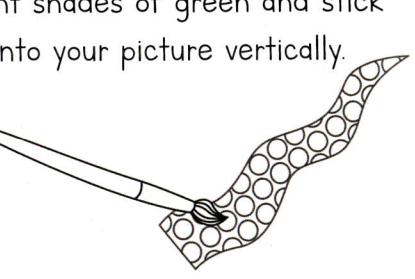

TIP Overlap the shapes to get a moving watery effect. You could even add a submarine if you like.

18 Make Shadow Puppets

You will need
A cardboard box
Paints
Brush
Tape
Scissors
Pencil
Black card
Tracing paper
Sticks
Glitter
Torch

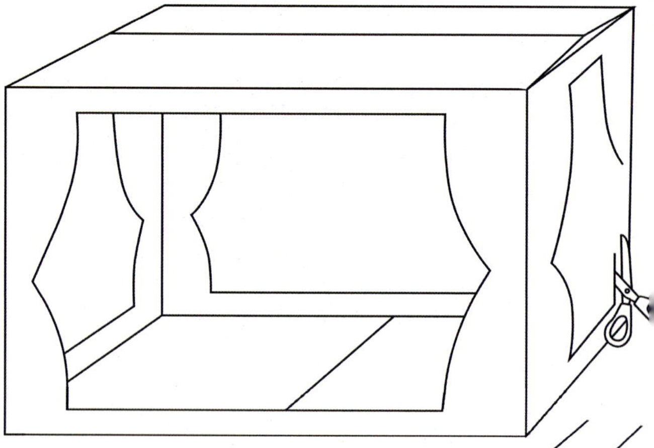

1 Cut out all four sides of the box. Leave some curtain shapes at the edges.

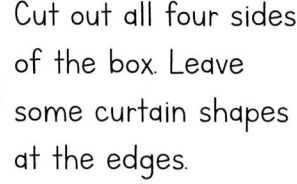

2 Paint the theatre a bright red.

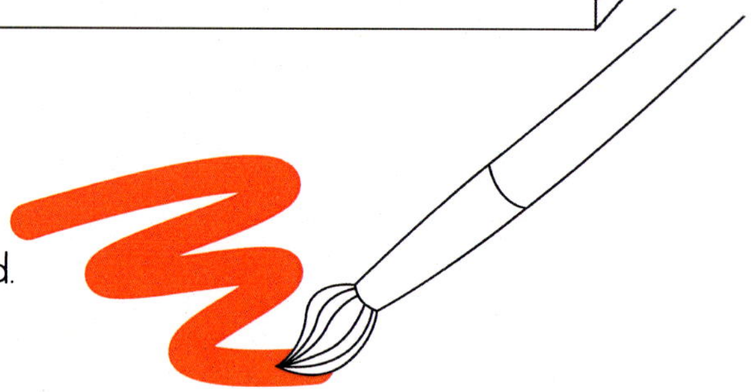

3 Make an arc for the top by cutting out a semi circle of card. Fold over a bit of the straight edge so it will stand up.

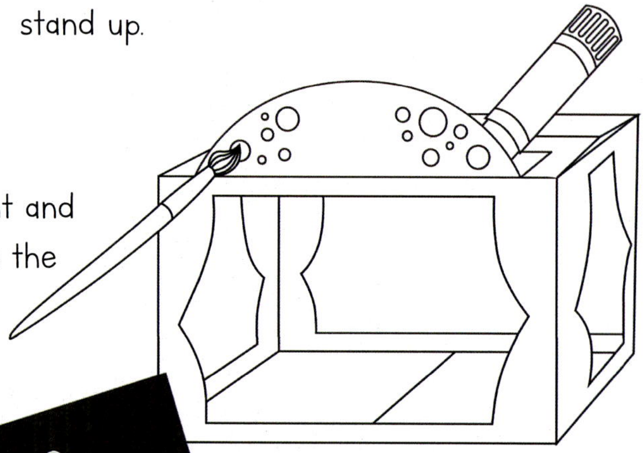

4 Decorate it with paint and glitter and then tape the folded bit to the top of the box.

5 Draw some animals shapes and people on the black card and cut them out. Tape them onto sticks.

6. Tape tracing paper onto the inside of the box at the front.

7. Shine a light from the back of the box onto the tracing paper.

Now you are ready to put on your play. Move the puppets around from the open sides of the box.

19 Make Tube People

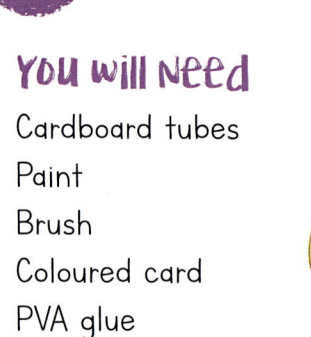

You will need
Cardboard tubes
Paint
Brush
Coloured card
PVA glue
Bits of material, ribbon, wool, buttons and beads
Pen

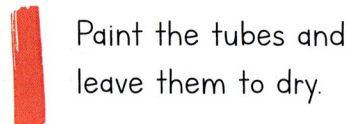

1 Paint the tubes and leave them to dry.

2 Cut out simple arms, hands and feet and stick them on.

3 Stick on bits of material to make clothes, wool for hair and buttons for eyes.

4 Add extra features with a pen.

20 Make a Wriggly Mobile

You will need

Two bamboo sticks
String
Cotton
Needle
Paper
Scissors
Coloured pens

1 Draw round a saucer onto the paper to get four circles. Cut them out.

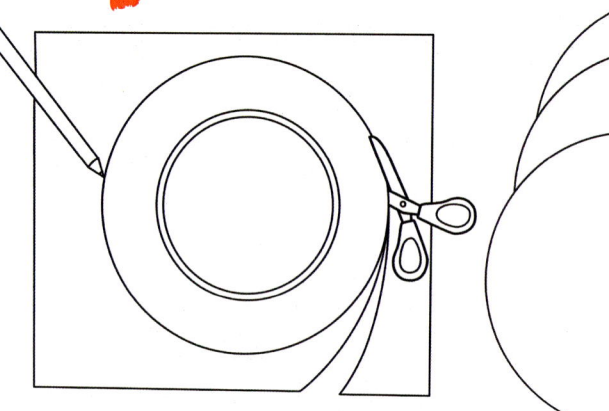
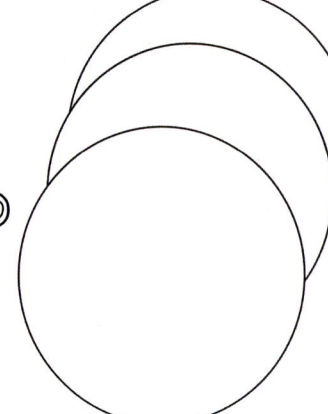

2 Using the pens, decorate the circles with snakey patterns.

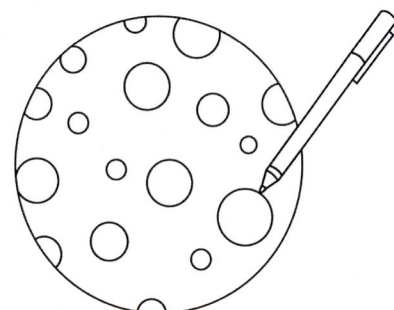

3 Draw a snake's head in the middle of the circle and then a line going round and round until you get to the edge.

Cut out the spiral. Do this three more times.

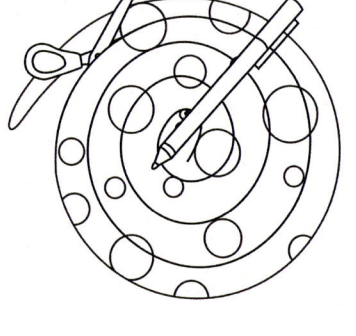
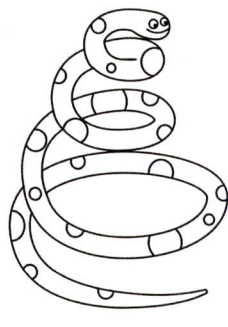

4 Tie the two sticks together to make a cross, leaving a long bit of string so that you can hang it up.

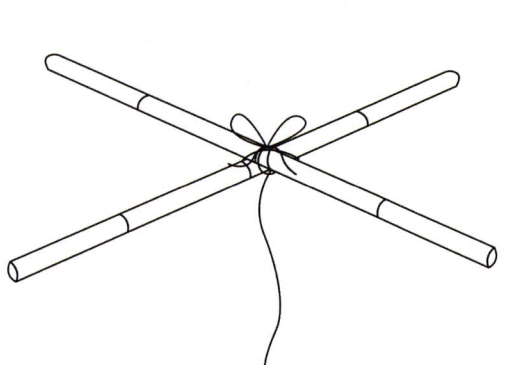

5 Thread the needle and tie a knot. Push the needle through a snake's head and tie it onto the end of one stick so that it dangles down.

6 Do this for each snake and then hang up your mobile.

21 and a wrigglier dragon

You will need
A long rod or stick
Paper plates
Cotton thread
Needle
Scissors
Strong glue
Buttons, corks, paper scraps, sequins

1 Draw round a saucer onto the paper to get four circles. Cut them out.

2 Decorate the first plate with a face and the other plates with body sections.

3 Thread the plates with cotton thread and tie them to the rod.

22 Make a Secret Code ...

Codes are a very useful way to keep information safe or to send secret messages to people. They can be made from numbers, letters or symbols.

You will need

Paper
Pens
Sticks or paper straws
Sticky tape
   ... and a friend or two

1 First make lots of flags with a friend.

These are easy to do by drawing lots of flags and then taping them to a stick or straw.

You must make two sets exactly the same so that you have a set each.

2 Then you must agree between you, the meaning of each flag.

Keep the meanings simple so that they are easy to remember such as:

>Do you want to play?
>Do you want to play hide and seek?
>Yes and No
>Let's meet in the kitchen!

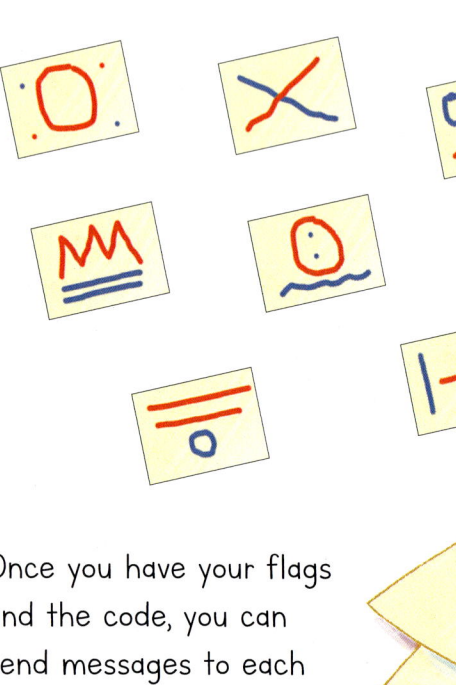

Once you have your flags and the code, you can send messages to each other without anybody else knowing what you are saying.

23 ... and treasure hunt codes

You will need
Paper
Pens
A friend and some treasure
  (This can be anything you like, it's a lovely way to give a friend a present.)

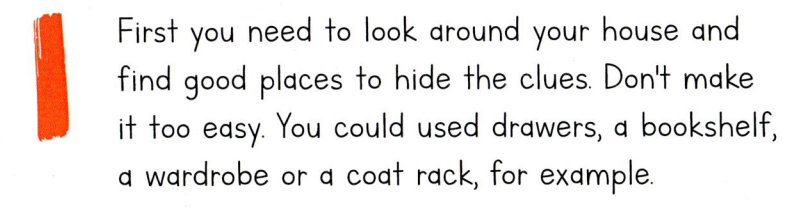

1 First you need to look around your house and find good places to hide the clues. Don't make it too easy. You could used drawers, a bookshelf, a wardrobe or a coat rack, for example.

2 Once you've found about 10 places, draw a picture of each one on a piece of paper.

3 Hide the treasure. Then hide the clues. The first clue you hide should be the picture of where the treasure is hidden. The next clue you hide should be the picture of where you hid the last clue. Work backwards to hide all the clues so that when your friend is trying to find the treasure, one clue will lead to the next.

24 MAKE DRIP PATTERNS

YOU WILL NEED
Thickly mixed paints
Thin paintbrushes
Sheet of white paper

1 Drip dots of different-coloured paints all over the paper, then blow gently across the sheet to smudge them.

25 MAKE COMB PATTERNS

YOU WILL NEED
Paints
Thin paste
White paper
Paintbrush
Old spoon
Old comb

1 Mix a jar of thick paint with a quarter of a jar of thin paste.

2 Spoon a little of the mixture onto the centre of the paper and use the comb to make swirly patterns all over the paper.

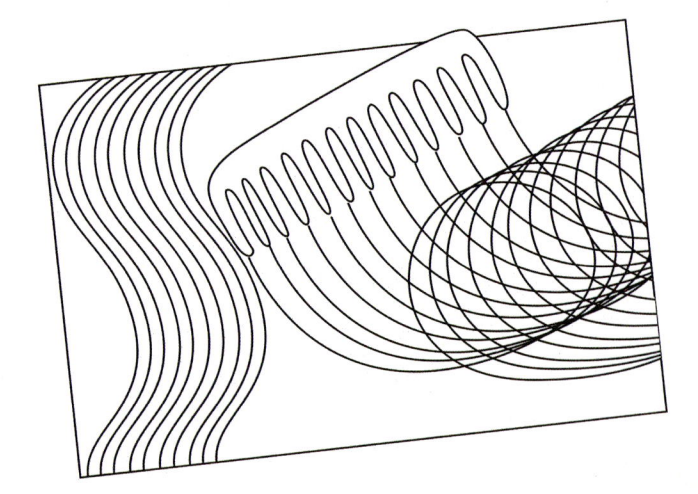

26 Make handprints

You will need
Paints
Large sheet of white paper
Paintbrush
Black pen

1 Paint your hand with thick paint and then press it down firmly on the piece of paper. Try making prints with the other hand, too.

2 Press more handprints over the paper, facing different ways and using other colours. Leave to dry.

TiP
When your prints are dry. You can create fun creatures by drawing faces, extra legs or hair on them with a black pen.

27 Make wax patterns

You will need
White paper
Cocktail stick
Coloured wax crayons
Water colour paints
Brush

1 Draw lots of squiggly lines and circles on the paper with the white crayon.

2 Then paint over them with very watery paints in lots of different colours.

The wax pattern will show through.

You can also make a wax scratch

Using lots of different-coloured wax crayons (but NOT the black wax crayon) cover a sheet of paper all over with colours.

Now cover the same sheet with black crayon.

Using a cocktail stick, scratch a picture in the black to remove the black wax, and show the colours below.

28 Make a Mirror Pattern

You will need
White paper
Water colour paints
Brush

1 Fold the sheet of paper in half and open it out again.

2 Using just two colours, paint a shape on one half of the paper only.

3 While the paint is still wet, fold the paper together again.

4 Press firmly and open the paper out to see your mirror pattern.

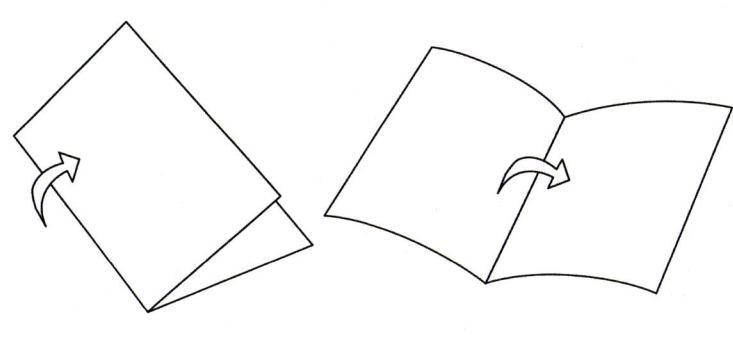

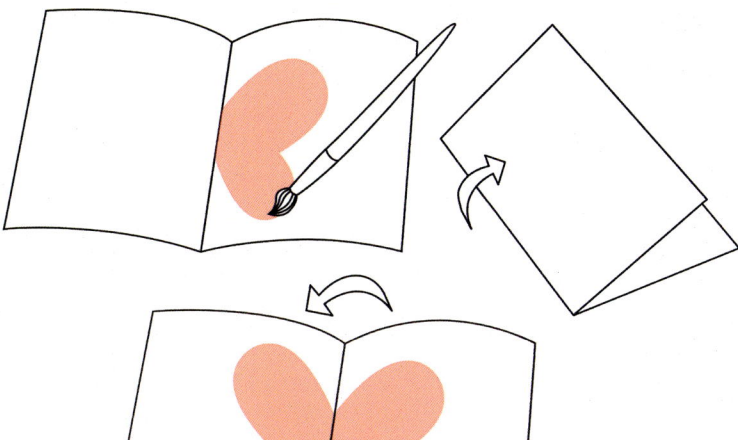

29 Make a Suncatcher

You will need

Scissors
Glue
Sheet of black paper
Paper plate
Yellow crayon
Sheets of coloured tissue paper
Length of string

1 Draw round the paper plate on the sheet of black paper using the yellow crayon or some white chalk.

2 Fold the circle in half and crease the fold. Then fold it again and once more.

3 Cut small shapes from the folded edges of the paper, taking care not to let these cuts overlap.

4 Open it out to see the pattern you have made.

5 Tear pieces of coloured tissue and paste them over the holes on one side of the black circle.

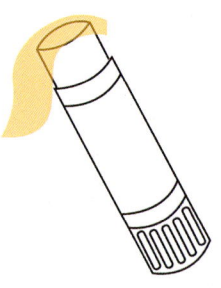

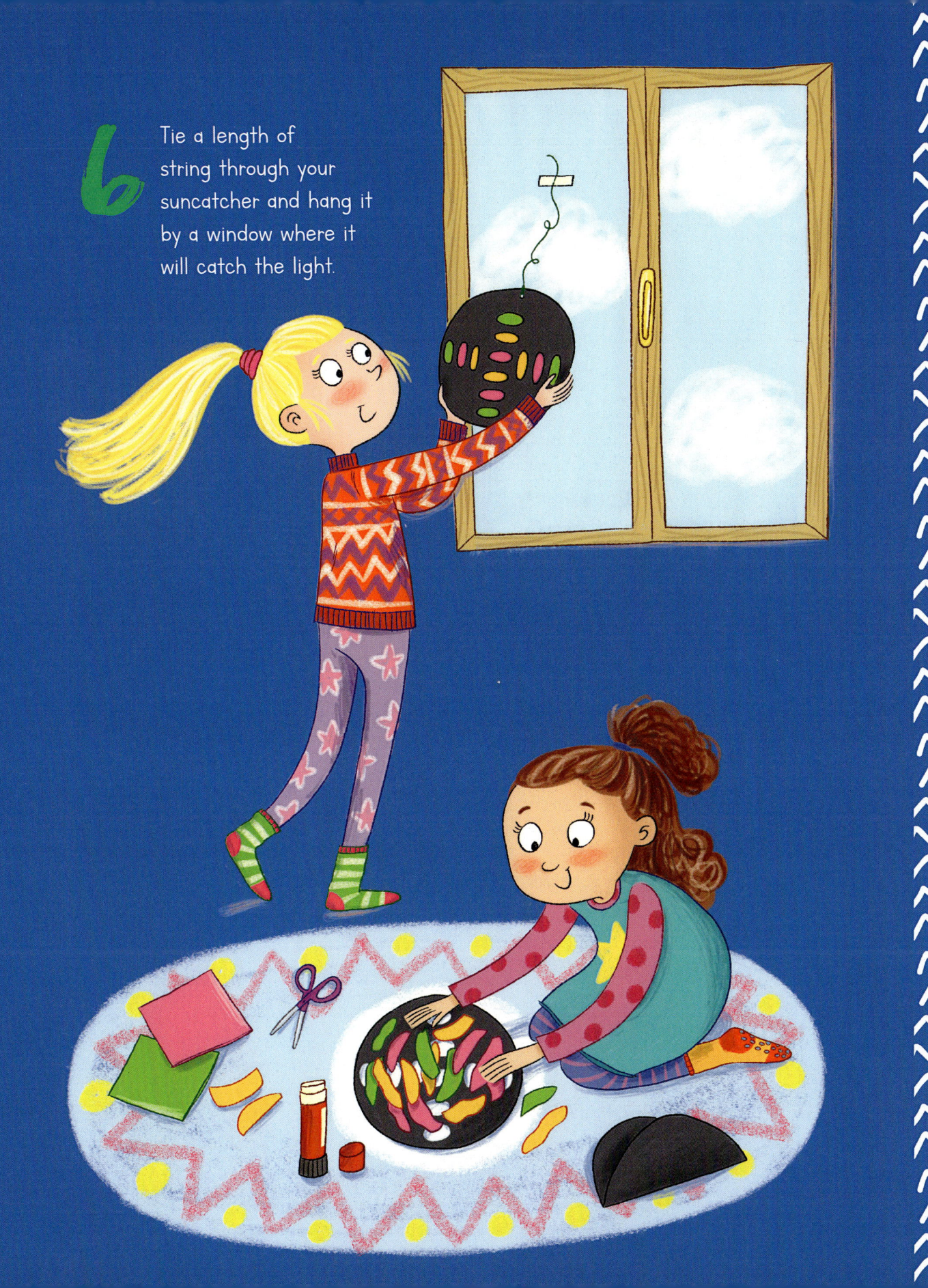

6 Tie a length of string through your suncatcher and hang it by a window where it will catch the light.

30 Make a Tangram

You will need
White paper
Scissors
Coloured crayons
Tracing paper

1 Trace this pattern exactly on a sheet of white paper. Colour each shape a different colour and cut each one out.

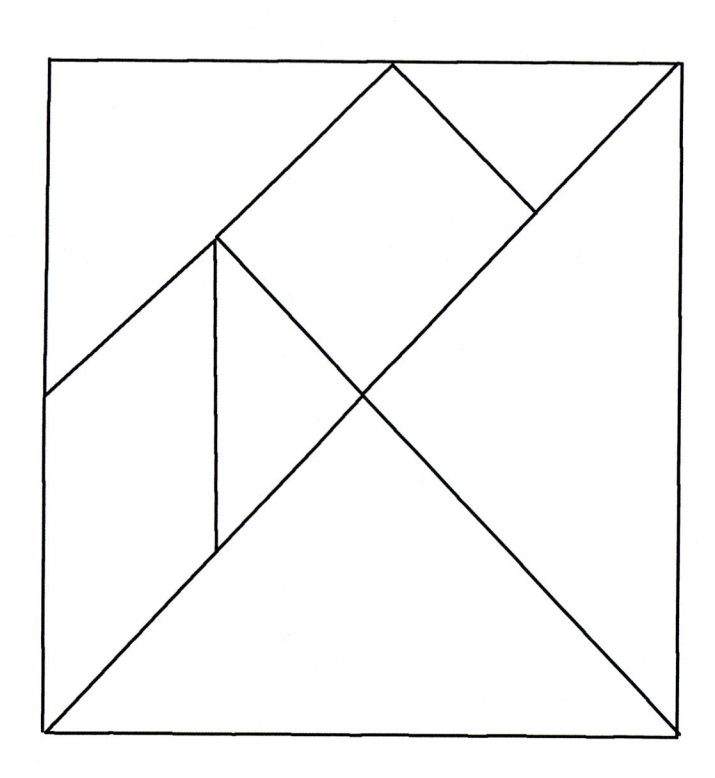

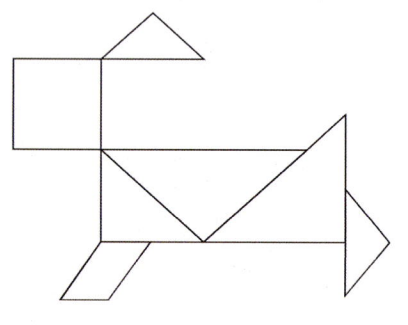

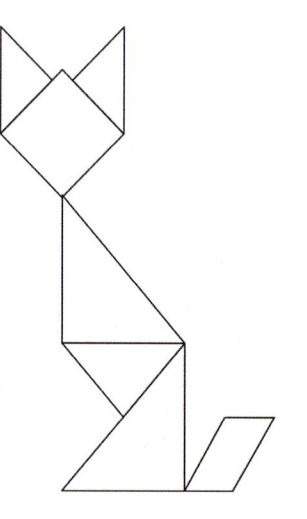

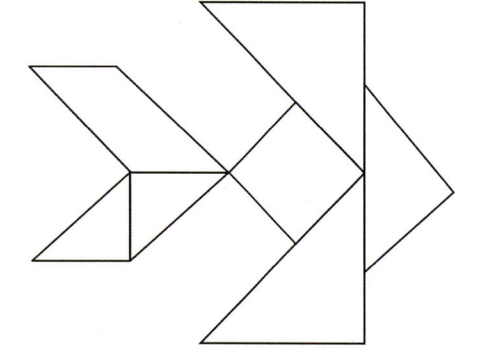

2 Make pictures and patterns using the shapes. Here are some ideas.

And some more ...

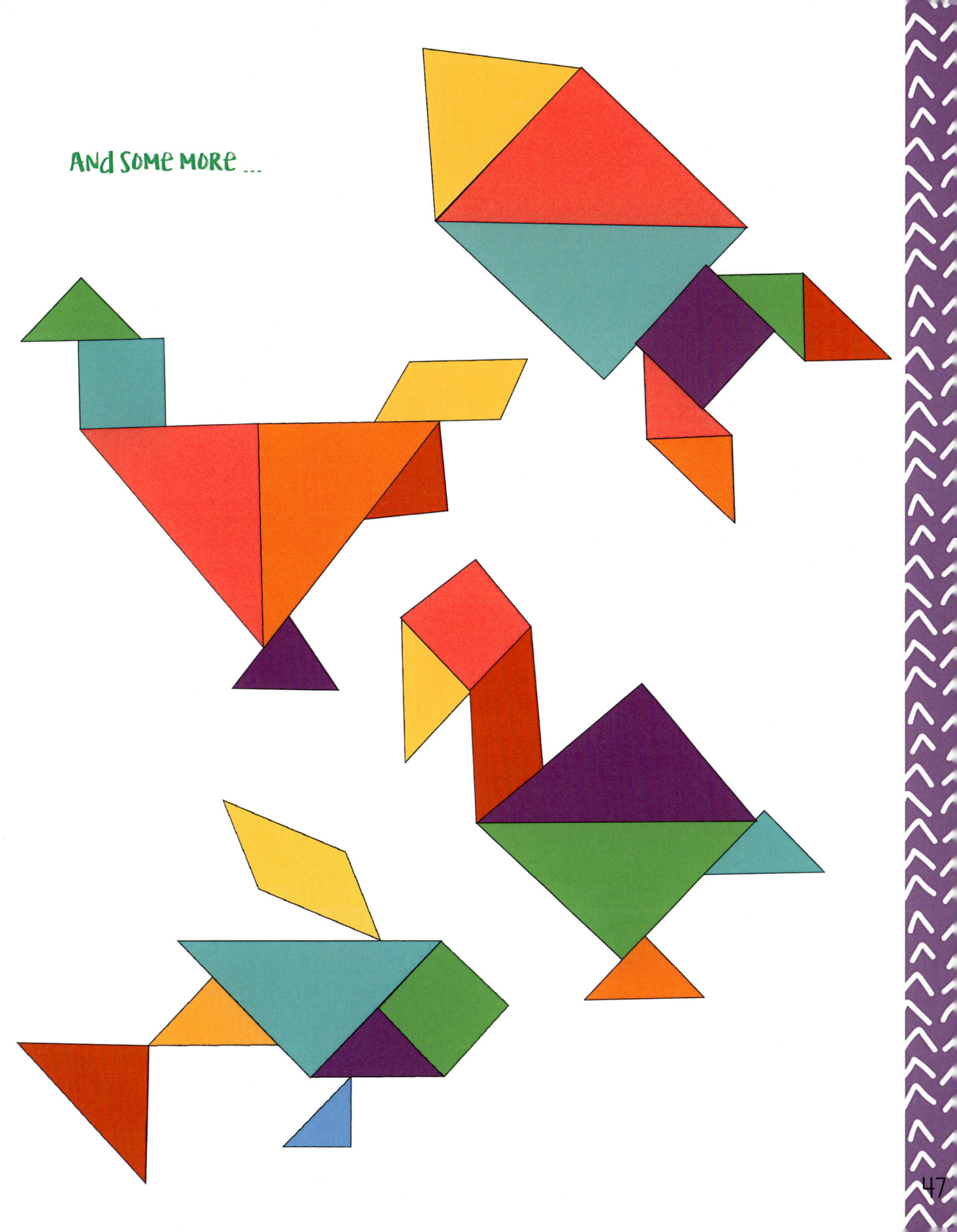

WRITTEN BY: FELICIA LAW

EDUCATIONAL TEXT: AIMÉE JACKSON

EDITORS: AIMÉE JACKSON; LUCY BRIGNALL

DESIGN: FELICIA LAW; IMRAN KELLY

COLOUR ILLUSTRATIONS: PAULINE REEVES (THE BRIGHT AGENCY)

ELISA ROCCHI (BEEHIVE ILLUSTRATION AGENCY)

BLACK LINE ILLUSTRATIONS: KERI GREEN (BEEHIVE ILLUSTRATION AGENCY)

P6-7 art MARTINA ROTONDO

COPYRIGHT © 2021 BrambleKids Ltd

ISBN: 978-1-914411-49-6